The M.D.'s Mistake

FASTBACK® Horror

The M.D.'s Mistake

BEN FARRELL

GLOBE FEARON
Pearson Learning Group

FASTBACK® HORROR BOOKS

The Caller	**The MD's Mistake**
The Disappearing Man	Night Games
The Hearse	Night Ride
Live Bait	No Power on Earth
The Lonely One	The Rare Shell
The Masterpiece	Tomb of Horror

All photography © Pearson Education, Inc. (PEI) unless specifically noted.

Copyright © 2004 by Pearson Education, Inc., publishing as Globe Fearon®, an imprint of Pearson Learning Group, 299 Jefferson Road, Parsippany, NJ 07054. All rights reserved. No part of this book may be reproduced or transmitted in any form or by any means, electronic or mechanical, including photocopying, recording, or by any information storage and retrieval system, without permission in writing from the publisher. For information regarding permission(s), write to Rights and Permissions Department.

Globe Fearon® and Fastback® are registered trademarks of Globe Fearon, Inc.

ISBN 0-13-024517-8
Printed in the United States of America
1 2 3 4 5 6 7 8 9 10   07 06 05 04 03

Globe Fearon
Pearson Learning Group

1-800-321-3106
www.pearsonlearning.com

Detective Paul Shapler was glad the mad dog matter was coming to an end. He rang Dr. Franklin's door bell. He could hear the chimes ringing inside the old house. For a brief moment Paul Shapler thought of walking away. But the sound of the door being unlocked fixed his mind on what he had to do. Then the door opened slightly.

"May I help you?" the bald man peeking out at the detective asked.

"Police Department," Detective Shapler answered, flashing his badge at the doctor. "I need to talk with you."

"Come in," the doctor said.

The puzzled look on the doctor's face surprised Paul. He'd expected the man to be frightened. He certainly had a good reason to be.

"Now what is it that you want?" Dr. Franklin asked after they'd seated themselves in the living room.

"Well, for a start, did you know Sandy Atkins? She was a nurse."

"Was?" the doctor repeated. "Did something happen to her?"

"She died about three weeks ago," Paul explained.

The doctor gasped. "How?" he asked quickly.

"I'll get to that later. You knew her?"

"Yes, I knew her. She worked with me a few times at the hospital. But that was years ago. I really haven't seen her in years. So why'd you come to see me? This doesn't have anything to do with me, does it?"

"That's what I'm here to find out," Paul said. "You could be the doctor we're looking for."

"Wait a minute. Are you telling me a doctor had something to do with her death?"

Paul Shapler glanced around the room. "We're alone?" he said, though he already knew the answer.

"My wife's gone away for a few days.

So, yes, we're alone. Is this something she shouldn't know about?"

"It certainly is," Paul replied, smiling slightly. "I mean it certainly is something she probably doesn't know about. You and Sandy Atkins had your little secret. And I don't think you shared it with your wife."

Anger showed on the doctor's face. "Listen," he said, "I worked with Sandy Atkins. I don't know what you're trying to hint at. And I'm not going to sit around here and try to guess."

"I'm talking about your work with her," Detective Shapler answered. "But we can get to that later. I suppose you heard that Dr. Gorman was bitten to death by a mad dog last week. You did know Dr. Gorman, didn't you?"

The mention of Gorman's name frightened the doctor. He raised his right hand to his mouth and nervously bit at one of his fingernails. "Ted Gorman was an old old friend of mine," he said softly. "I'd worked with him at the hospital, and we'd been friends even before then. I was shocked to hear that he was dead. It was such a horrible way to die."

"Yes," Paul agreed. "His face was almost eaten away."

The terror in Dr. Franklin's eyes pleased Paul. It wouldn't be long before he'd be telling the whole story.

"And you think all of this has something to do with me?" the doctor said.

"I think you have something to do with it. But maybe if I go back to the beginning, you'll be able to understand this better. Years ago you and Dr. Gorman and Sandy Atkins worked together at the hospital. You handled emergencies. And one emergency tied you together in a special way. Do you remember that one?"

Just then the telephone rang. "I have to answer that," Dr. Franklin said.

"Go ahead," Paul told him. "But I don't think it would be wise for you to mention that I'm here."

"I wasn't planning to mention a thing," the doctor answered as he headed for the phone in the next room.

Paul wandered over to the front window. There wasn't a person on the street. It was a nice, quiet neighborhood. Paul raised his hand to the lock on the window. The lock was old. It was probably as old as the house. But it turned easily. "What are you doing?" the doctor asked, as he stepped back into the living room.

Paul turned around quickly. "Just checking to see if you were worried about crime in this neighborhood," he said. "I gather you trust our police force."

"I'm worried about what you're getting at," the doctor said.

Paul returned to his seat facing the doctor. "Yeah," he said, "let's get back to that emergency."

"Listen, I don't have all night. And I

don't know what you're talking about."

"Okay," Paul shrugged, "but stop me whenever you want. About a month ago Sandy Atkins showed up at the station house. She was frightened for her life. Anyhow, I got to talk to her."

"What was she frightened about?"

"She didn't really want to tell. She'd seen a man on the street and the sight of him frightened her. The funny thing was that she couldn't explain why. That was what she told me. And that was why I told her I couldn't help her. We don't go after people without a reason. Finally, she told me the guy's name. I was surprised to hear it because I know the guy. He's a gentle fellow. I even told her so. But she was sure he wasn't going to be gentle with her.

"Why not?" the doctor asked.

"She thought he wanted to get even with her. Some years earlier he'd been hurt and brought to the hospital. He was in bad shape, and an emergency operation was performed on him. She and two doctors were there for the operation. The guy was in high school at the time. He had been hurt in a football game. Until that night, a lot of colleges wanted him. Not only was he a good football player; he was also smart. After that night he was never the same. His brain was damaged."

"Are you talking about Carl Walker?" Dr. Franklin asked.

"I thought you'd be able to guess that."

"Well I certainly remember him," the doctor said. "He came in with a terrible head injury. Dr. Gorman saved his life.

I'm sure of that. I know the young man wasn't the same, but he was lucky to be alive."

"Sandy Atkins told the same story at first. But once she saw I wasn't going to help her, she changed her tune. She said that Carl Walker's brain had been damaged during the operation. She said the operation had been messed up. And she said that you and Gorman and she were in on it."

The doctor tried to laugh, but it was a weak try. "It sounds as if Sandy were in need of a doctor."

"In a way she was," Paul said. "I mean there was no way for Carl Walker to know what you and the others had done to him. He isn't smart now like he was in high school."

"How do you know?" Dr. Franklin asked.

"I knew him in high school. I can remember how he was before the operation. And I know how he's been since then."

"The operation wasn't messed up," the doctor said, trying to look as truthful as he could. "And even if it had been messed up, there's nothing that can be done about it now."

"I guess not," Paul answered. "And besides, you're the only one left."

"What do you mean by that? Are you trying to tell me that Carl Walker is after me? Or, do you think *I* had something to do with these deaths?"

"I think you had something to do with Carl Walker's operation."

"I don't understand this. Why didn't you help Sandy?"

"There was no way to help her. About a week after she came to see me Sandy Atkins died of a heart attack. It turns out she had a history of heart trouble. And seeing Carl Walker after all these years probably put too much of a strain on her," Paul said.

"Are you sure there was no foul play involved?" the doctor asked anxiously. "People have been known to kill other people and make it look like a heart attack."

"And who do you have in mind for a suspect?"

"What about Carl?" the doctor asked.

"He wasn't there," Paul said. "I had gone over to his place that night. In fact, it's funny that I was talking to him just about the time she had her heart attack."

"And you call that funny?" the doctor said.

"I don't mean it was something to laugh about. But it was funny that I was talking to Carl right at that time. There was no need to bring him in for questioning. He couldn't have been at Sandy's place."

"Maybe he sent someone else there."

"Maybe," Paul agreed, "but let's get back to the operation. Suppose I tell you what Dr. Gorman had to say."

"Gorman?" the doctor gasped, "you talked to him before he died?"

"Sure. I wanted to see if there was anything to the story Sandy Atkins had told me. Well, he said that nothing had gone wrong in the operation. And he didn't believe her idea that Carl was after her. Or you. Or him. In fact, he went for a ride with me to see Carl at his job. And Carl didn't even recognize him."

"Why didn't you come to see me after that?" Dr. Franklin asked.

"That was my first thought," Paul said. "But Gorman had a change of heart after he saw Carl. We were riding back to his place in my car when he broke down. I guess seeing Carl made him feel bad. He told me all about the operation. He even told me about your mistake. And about how the three of you had agreed to keep the whole thing a secret."

"That's a lie," Dr. Franklin cried out. "You can't get me to admit to any of that."

Paul shrugged. "It really doesn't make any difference. Even if you did ruin Carl's life, no one can put you in jail for it. I suppose you could have been sued at the time of the operation. But it's probably too late for that. Both of Carl's parents are dead now. They were heartbroken about him. But they were just poor people. Gorman knew that. He told me he even once suggested giving them some money to help Carl get some kind of training. But you didn't want any part of that. You wanted to keep your hands clean."

"Stop it!" the doctor cried out. "I'll tell you the whole thing."

"Go on," Paul said. "I'm listening."

"It was a busy day in that emergency room. I can't remember all the cases we handled. But I can remember that I was tired. I suppose I should have said that I was too tired, but I didn't. Anyway, after the operation was over, I had to watch Carl's life signs. I was sitting next to the operating table, watching him. But I guess I dozed off for a moment. Sandy woke me up. Then Gorman returned. Carl had lost some oxygen to the brain.

"We knew his brain might have been damaged," the doctor continued. "But we hoped he was going to be all right. And we agreed that we'd keep my falling asleep a secret, however Carl came out of it. Well, you know the rest. It was just a horrible thing. Believe me, I'll never forget it."

"Why didn't you go along with Gorman and try to help Carl get some training?"

"Gorman was crazy," Dr. Franklin said calmly. "How would that have looked? It would have been like we were saying that we knew a mistake had been made.

Besides, I had the most to lose. I was the one who fell asleep."

"Carl was the one who lost," Paul Shapler said, staring hard at the doctor.

"Listen," the doctor answered, "what do you want from me? I made a mistake. Didn't you ever make a mistake? I read about the police making mistakes all the time. Well, doctors make mistakes, too. If I were you, I'd be trying to find out who, if anyone, killed Sandy and Gorman. And if you think I had something to do with their deaths, then take me in. But if not, I think we've come to the end of this talk."

Paul Shapler shook his head. "No," he said, "I don't think you had anything to do with their deaths. Oh, sure, they both knew your secret. But I don't think you'd kill them or hire anyone else to do it. So, you're right, this is the end of our little talk."

"What about the mad dog?" the doctor asked.

"We caught him tonight," Paul said. "He was just a wild dog. As far as we know, no one owned him. How he happened to attack Dr. Gorman is anybody's guess. Anyway, the dog is locked up in the animal shelter. So you have nothing to worry about."

The doctor jumped out of his seat. "You get out of here," he said, pointing at the front door. "And if you ever tell anyone about that operation, I'll see that you get kicked off the police force. You have some nerve coming here and scaring me to death. You weren't doing your duty. Now get out!"

Paul started to say something, but decided against it. At the door he turned and looked at the doctor. "You never talked to me," the doctor whispered. "Just remember that."

"I will," Paul answered. "You can be sure of that."

Paul's car was parked down the street. When he reached it, he glanced back at the doctor's house. Franklin was standing in the doorway. Paul smiled and slid into the driver's seat.

Franklin really was scared. He was scared about his secret.

As Paul pulled away from the curb, he could feel the anger boiling inside him. Franklin was the worst of the three of them. The other two had told *all* of the truth. With help, they'd said, they probably could have gotten Carl back to normal. But Franklin had talked them out of getting help. He'd talked them into their secret plan.

The old days flashed through Paul's mind. He remembered his freshman year in high school. He and Carl had been the last two players to make the football team. They both knew that, and in a way, they'd become friends because of it.

By their sophomore year they'd become

best friends. Kids in their classes used to tease them about their being together all the time. "You guys must be going steady," they used to say.

Carl got hurt in a game during their junior year. Paul had missed a block, and Carl had gotten slammed. They'd carried him off the field and taken him away to the hospital. Paul remembered how he had thrown up right on the field.

Paul also remembered how he'd quit the team after seeing what had happened to his friend. In a way, he had quit life. He kept to himself and didn't make any new friends. He couldn't stop blaming himself for what had happened to his friend.

Day after day, he'd stopped at Carl's house and tried to talk to him. He remembered hoping for some kind of miracle to make Carl normal again. But Carl was *never* going to be normal again.

When Paul reached home, Carl was waiting. "Did you eat?" Paul asked.

"I eat with you," Carl answered, giving Paul a sad smile.

Paul couldn't eat. He picked at his food and watched Carl. He wasn't sorry he'd taken Carl in after Carl's parents were gone. Carl was still his best friend. And those three people had wrecked his life. They'd wrecked Paul's life, too. Well, a miracle had happened. Two of them had been paid back for what they had done to Carl.

A little later, Paul told Carl, "I'm going out. You go ahead and go to sleep."

When Paul pulled into a parking space around the corner from Dr. Franklin's house, the street was quiet. He was glad all the people in the neighborhood went to bed early. He was especially glad Dr. Franklin did.

He quietly walked across the doctor's lawn to the front window. Gently, he tested it. It was still unlocked. The doctor hadn't bothered to check it. Paul slowly raised the window. It made no noise. Then, just as slowly, he climbed inside.

About five minutes later, Detective Paul Shapler climbed out of Dr. Franklin's front window. Then he listened carefully. He could hear no sounds in the house. His eyes searched the street. It was calm. The whole street was sleeping.

When Paul reached his car, he remembered telling Franklin about the mad dog. He remembered saying, "Anyway, the dog is locked up in the animal shelter."

Paul smiled. Like Franklin, he hadn't told *all* of the story. The wild dog had been caught. Paul had helped to catch him. And Paul had promised to drop him off at the animal shelter.

Paul glanced up the street. He didn't want any passing cars to see him. But it was quiet. He opened the trunk lid of his car. The muzzled dog jumped up at Paul, but the chain flipped him back into the trunk. "You don't want me," Paul whispered. "But I have someone else for you. He's sleeping like a baby."

Slowly, Paul untied the chain and pulled the dog out of the trunk. He was going to have to think of one more story tomorrow. He was going to have to explain how the dog had escaped—and claimed another victim.